Only Built 4 Champagne Thoughts…

Copyright © 2017 Eric Walton
All Rights Reserved
ISBN-13: 978-1976188664
ISBN-10: 1976188660

# Fresh Grapefruit
## (The Preluded Epilogue)

Remember this
It shall replenish…

There's a difference between being alone and being set apart
Former is a state of mind
Latter is a state of grace
The heart suffers or strives
Depending on one or the other

You're not alone
You're where you said you will
You're who you are
You're never forgotten, never will
No matter the lack of voices
No matter if they matter
Matter of fact…

They matter not in this matter
Unless you make them matter

Enjoy this time amongst the clouds
You've come so far
And arrived
But…

This is only temporary
This is time being…
As all is this planet
And the universe

Why reach for the clouds
When you can touch the stars…

# Champagne Mimosa Mornings

You have ascended on high…

You have received gifts among men…

# Bagels with the Smoked Salmon Cream Cheese

Knowledge comes from learning
Wisdom comes from living

Fear comes from living the learned in a continuous loop…
The reversion of applying knowledge obtained before the wisdom
bore understanding to fruition

The fear of the unknown is a few things…
Mainly a byproduct of one
The one thing is a lack of discipline
There can be understanding
Yet discipline isn't guaranteed
There can be structure
Yet without discipline
Totally useless

Patience is an extension of discipline in a lot of ways
Patience doesn't exist without discipline
A lack of discipline is a lack of patience
A lack of patience is a lack of understanding
A lack of understanding is a total disregard of wisdom

Wisdom comes from living
Wisdom isn't said to come from lived
The present is all that matters
The gift is wrapping up the past and leaving it there for
understanding to give birth to supreme knowledge
Knowledge comes from learned is nothing but an excuse…
Excuses never amount to discipline
Excuses are a lack of advancement
Excuses are a lack of wisdom
And lacking wisdom is knowledge never being born
Knowledge never being born is understanding never existing

Understanding bring value to life
Understanding is valuable knowledge
Discipline is a result of your understanding
Discipline is a result of your will

There is the problem...

Discipline is a result of acquired wisdom
Discipline rests in being wise
The wisest have done unwise things
Ask King Solomon
And King Solomon asked for and received wisdom directly from God
As if asking for a glass of water to quench his thirst
That leads to another conundrum of sorts...

King Solomon was wise in asking for wisdom
But how could he ask for something that he didn't have
Again...King Solomon was wise to ask for wisdom

How can one be wise without wisdom?

King Solomon couldn't receive if he didn't already possess
Follow the flow...

If we don't have knowledge of something
Then does that mean that something doesn't exist?
If I never met anyone
If I never came across an individual
Then is that individual nonexistent
Even if there is record of existence
Social Security Number
Birth Certificate
Current Address
Place of Employment

The person exists
Our knowledge of the person's existence does not...

If this holds true with a stranger
Then how much more with ourselves
Even more so with matters of elevation
Growth and Development

King Solomon knew he was king

Rather he was AWARE
This awareness then led to learning
He then learned his kingship
He processed his learning
He was living as king

God came forth to him and gave a request
King Solomon living as king went off what he knew…
I am now king
I need to know more than what I know
I need to understand how to have those understand why I am king
I need to understand myself
I need wisdom to gain such understanding
I need understanding to give myself the greatest value of being king

King Solomon had the awareness that led to learned knowledge
King Solomon was wise to ask for wisdom

Therefore, learned knowledge leads to becoming wise
Applying learned knowledge is how you become wise
King Solomon applied his knowledge
King Solomon was wise

King Solomon as wise to ask for wisdom

This shows discipline rests in being wise
More so discipline rests in wisdom
The wise can do unwise things
The wise can lose wisdom

A lack of knowledge is not a lack of discipline
A lack of knowledge cannot know of discipline
Discipline is a learned attribute
Knowledge comes from learning
No knowledge, no discipline

The truth if any matter is not your truth necessarily
Someone else's truth can be a total lie
This holds truth with a lack of discipline

Discipline covers a multitude
Discipline saves one from self
Discipline makes one suited for enlightenment
Discipline spurs growth and development

Lack of discipline leads to unwise moments
Self-correction recognizes such
Self-improvement realizes such

Therefore, there can be discipline in one matter and the lack of discipline in yet another
One must learn both
Learning the lack of discipline is becoming knowledgeable of that matter
Knowledge comes from learning
The recognition of this lack of discipline gave way to removing such
This is self-correction

The application of the new knowledge is how you become wise…
You don't become wise to the lack of discipline
You become wise in improving discipline
You then seek wisdom to build and strengthen discipline
You not only realize the need to improve discipline
You constantly refine and replenish your discipline
You realize the constant need for discipline
You realize the benefits of discipline
This is self-improvement

There is a reason that you only have one mouth
Yet you have two ears and two eyes
You learn by listening
You live by seeing
You learn by seeing
You learn by living

This says that you need to listen and see twice more than you speak
This says to watch words carefully
This says to listen to words carefully
Yours and others
This says to make yours words meaningful and significant

Seeing that you have one mouth being heard

Not every question spoken needs to be heard
Not every answer heard needs to be spoken

Not every answer spoken needs to be heard
Not every question heard needs to be spoken

Discipline accomplishes such refrain
Wisdom establishes such refrain

The existence of patience is an existence of discipline
Patience is a result of discipline
Patience strengthens discipline
Patience never exists without discipline
A lack of patience is a lack of discipline

Lack of patience, lack of wisdom
That's definite
No patience, no knowledge
That's a conundrum

Take Abraham for instance…
Did God not give knowledge of a child?
Did God make aware?
Did Abraham receive such knowledge?
Did God make Abraham aware?
With that said, did Abraham not plant seed leading to the enemy of his own?
This was due to a lack of patience
This lack of patience has nothing to do with a lack of knowledge

Having patience is having discipline
However, there are moments when patience wears thin
You then must have discipline not to sin
You then must have discipline to do the right thing
You then must rely on wisdom

Wisdom never dies
Wisdom never fades

Wisdom can be lost by us
Wisdom never loses

We lose patience
We shouldn't lose wisdom along the way
Discipline helps awareness amongst lack of patience
Self-awareness is an acquisition of knowledge of self
You must be aware of self and everything else
Knowledge is awareness
We can lack awareness
We can't lose knowledge
Knowledge exists whether we are aware or knowledgeable…
Or not

So, then what is the true matter of awareness
Awareness is becoming wise
Becoming wise to someone, something, somewhere…
A lack of patience does not coincide with a lack of knowledge
A lack of patience can lead to a lack of wisdom
However, discipline is the very thing to refresh
More so revive the lack of wisdom
Needed to do the right thing
The wise thing…
The wise thing is the right thing
The wise thing is the proper thing

Adam and Eve
The epitome of the saying "Ignorance is bliss"
Adam was formed in God's image
Adam was given dominion over everything
Adam even rested on the 7th
Adam was forbidden to eat from the True of Knowledge
Therefore, did lack knowledge?

Remember King Solomon
He was wise to ask for wisdom
Therefore, he obtained what was already possessed

This leads to Adam…
This is a conundrum

The fact is simple…
Adam possessed wisdom
Adam possessed divine wisdom
That being a special kind of wisdom
A wondrous wisdom
Adam's wisdom was limitless
Adam's wisdom was unfathomable

Adam lost this wisdom when he ate from The Tree
In gaining knowledge on the ground level
He gained awareness of the ground level
The ground level knowledge was awakened
Adam obtained what was possessed
Adam's wisdom was now then limited
Adam's sin limited his wisdom

This shows three things:
More so proves them…
Adam suffered from lack of discipline
The lack discipline spurred a lack of patience
No discipline, no knowledge
No patience, no awareness despite knowledge existing

His "ignorance" was a time of bliss
His acquired knowledge was not

Despite such, we live to see tomorrow
We live to learn
We learn to live

The beauty of structure rests in the beauty of God
God created 70 languages beautifully
When man wasn't acting beautifully
This one done to stop man from attacking structure
In essence, this provided 70 ways to communicate
This provided 70 ways to learn about the next person different from you
This provided 70 different ways to learn to about God
This provided 70 ways to communicate God
This created 70 different attributes to focus on God

This created 70 names of God

From the conspiring at the structure
We received 70 structures
This also reflects the beauty of Adam
From one man molded in God's image
We have many men well thereafter who are different

Structure is all about giving direction
Structure is put in place to make sense of where you need to go
Structure is put in place where you should go
Structure is the confidence
Structure is the comfort
Structure is the very faith to explain and to soothe the heart
Structure is the guideline for the spirit
Structure strengthens the spirit
Structure is the means to encourage the best in everything
Structure speaks to be proper and just
Structure is put in place to make us accountable to God and others
Structure can always exist without the lack of discipline
Structure is reliant of discipline
The lack of discipline renders structure useless
More like null and void
Selfishness obliterates structure
Selfishness is a lack of discipline
You can sit in a church
You can sit in a mosque
You can sit in a synagogue
If you are selfish in your acts…
If you lack discipline in your walk…
You can sit in all three different structures every day
For as long as you live…
Truth will set others free
And confine you to condemnation

Structure is the foundation set to treat others justly and hold you accountable
Structure is the means to motivation to further your walk
Structure gives the direction along your walk and proper actions
Structure is not the right path to enlightenment

But it also enlightens the right path
For you to see where to be

Structure is the highest form of discipline

The First Temple was the greatest structure constructed
The First Temple fell due to lack of discipline
The Second Temple was another in the greatest structures constructed
The Second Temple fell due to a lack of discipline

If these walls could talk…
Fear not
We have flesh and blood examples who can speak to this also
The difference is in the discipline and patience

Adam lacked discipline
Adam fell

Jesus never lacked discipline
Jesus rose… never fell off the cross

To further the conversation in case doubt arises…
One can say Jesus became impatient
The lack of patience in His own words…
"My God. My God. Why You forsaken Me?"
This was the 9$^{th}$ hour
This is not a lack of patience
This is a warm embrace of fulfilling His purpose
Reaping His reward sown from discipline He maintained and shown
This is the moment where He atoned for every man, woman, child
For every sin…
For every judgement…
This being He set us free

Jesus rose… never fell

Therefore, we can equate the following… now the obvious:
Discipline and patience results in obedience
Structure is the measurement of obedience

Jesus is the supreme measurement of obedience
Jesus is the supreme measurement of knowledge
Jesus is the supreme measurement of wisdom

To understand Jesus is to understand everything

Jesus teaches forever so we can keep learning
Jesus lives forever so we can keep living

Have no fear

Knowledge comes from learning
Wisdom comes from living

Peace…

# Fresh Flowers

The story of a rose amongst its collective… and amongst self

Roses come to being within a garden
Roses come together in a vase
The time shred and unity displayed is of a resplendent beauty
The collective is refreshing to the spirit when beheld
The resplendence to the senses is stupendous

Commonly roses are associated by the dozen in commonplace
The roses are always seen in the collective
This is second nature
Naturally they are seen sharing the same collective light
They are seen in the same collective light
They are associated automatically
This is second nature

Second nature sees similarities
First nature differences

Amongst this shared collective is an individual difference
The study of the roses by the dozen…
Some take well to the light and flourish
Some take decent to the light and manage
Some take not so well to the light and survive
Some take nothing as if it is flat out refusal

Second nature sees this as a problem…
Not understanding this is quite fine naturally
As this is first nature…

The commonplace is to see the commonality and commonly
commence concerted efforts to make everything common…
Ignoring the individual differences
Ignoring the individual
Such is the nature with the story of the rose…

So the story continues…
Unfortunately this is all too common

The roses that take not so well and take nothing
These are places directly with the decent and flourishing
The gap is closed between the groups
The thought process being second nature…
If these doing decent and flourishing are such
Then the not so well and nothing can get the same and become as them…

The next day or so…
The decent and flourishing ones show decline
They slowly lose signs of life
They begin withering away…

The rose slowly dies…

Now how is that so when they not only come up tougher but shared the same light

The first level of understanding…
Sharing is not the same as receiving

True each rose as a collective share the same source of light
More so has the same accessibility to the same source of light
The environment is the vase and water
The collective lives the same environment
However, each rose still doesn't receive the light the same
The differences in the degrees of life display this truth

In truth, the second level of understanding is the most important lesson…
As one receives, one reflects

The life of the rose is the reflection of the light it receives
From this we know not every rose receives the light the same

The third level of understanding arises from the second…
The fact that each rose has an individual connection with the light
This connection can be deterred
And even destroyed

Is the light then stolen
This light in question is not the light of the source
This is the light of the rose
The sheer reflection of the light
This is the energy of the rose
This is a life force to which the rose gives and receives
This is how the rose lives
This is life

Energy is a reflection of the light
Energy more so is a reflection of the life
The difference is energy is measured whether one is striving or surviving

With this supreme knowledge, we now understand the proper resolution…
The crux of the matter:
The difference of the individual rose is its uniqueness
Despite being part of a collective of commonalities, you grow apart
The rose was cultivated with others during growth collectively
The rose needs separate cultivation from others for growth individually
One who receives the light properly gives sensational energy
One who doesn't receive the light properly takes away

The rose removed and moved moves forward

The Lord lets its flourish…

# Dogfights with the Red Baron

Life is not difficult
Life is knowledge

Those who are ignorant can rectify such
Make life easier for self
Those who are stupid cannot be absolved
For having knowledge yet disregarding knowledge
Or being one who willfully ignores knowledge despite being knowledgeable
This one makes relationships with others difficult

A sheep can cry wolf oh so many times before the cries are disregarded
Until the wolf is there and death is imminent
For the cries fall on deaf ears
Such is the same for those dwelling in stupidity
Those who constantly refuse and reject words of wisdom
Those who reject upstanding and outstanding understanding
The supreme counsel of the wise

For whom amongst you desire to continue to waste love upon those who waste life

The chances you take reflect the choices you make
Choose life, such choice is the following:

Seek education
Share intelligence
Show discipline

Change and transform

Understanding the difference is to know the difference
The wisdom of the difference brings the understanding
Therefore, I shall provide the knowledge
And the wisdom that rests within
Thus I provide the chance to seek education and receive intelligence
To gain knowledge and remove ignorance

Furthermore, show discipline properly in gaining understanding

If you think changing and transforming are one of the same
Then heed the fact that you do not know
Act accordingly
Choose wisely
Be humble to seek education
In such you seek clarity

If you believe change and transform are one of the same
Remove your presence from my eyes
Your gift is unacceptable in my sight
We cannot see eye to eye

Now the time to share intelligence:
To think and to believe are different acts
One is an act of assimilation
The other a state of rest by renewal
Such is the case with changing and transforming
Conformity versus completion
The fine line between deceit and development

Let's bring this to a close:
The chance is there
The choice is yours
God gives free will
Yet still wants His will to instill
To do His will is to be right
Being right and being perfect are different
God is perfect
Jesus the same
So is the Spirit
As such is love
The love which is for the rise
The love which perfects
If you choose life
As choosing life is choosing wisely
Understand
You shall as you will

So strive for perfection
That isn't being perfect
That is being right

# Wavy Days

So you want to know why we all go through certain ebbs and flows?
Let's do the knowledge and grab the wisdom from what's there…

We are a threefold creation…
We are made in His image
We are molded out of His dust
We are given life by His breath

That's 3
100% represents completion as we know it

So that 3 is 30%
This is deduced due to the next statement of fact

We are 70% water
The earth is 70% water
"We are molded out of His dust" …

The answer rests in the wisdom of the water
This is your understanding…

Water takes form of whatever container
If you pour water into a glass
It becomes the glass
It takes form of the glass

If you pour water into a bucket
It becomes the bucket
It takes form of the bucket

If you throw water across the floor
It becomes the floor
It takes form of the floor

The water is the worldly
The water is good enough to quench thirst
And it's bad enough to pull you under and drown you

The key is the 30% navigating the 70%
The 30% will save you from drowning
The 30% will steer you clear

Sail free…

Keep your head above all
Keep your mind clear
It's already in your heart to do so

The heart is where it starts
The mind is where you find…

Let me expand on this thought:

The heart is where everything shall start
But you will find that the biggest influence is the mind

A polluted mind renders the heart null and void
The mind can constantly attack the heart
The stress from such can cause a heart attack
A heart attack is the heart fighting back
It is fighting back against the struggle and torment
It is fighting to stay afloat
It is fighting to rise above
The spirit is struggling to strive
The spirit shall always succeed
It shall succeed at the expense of the body
It shall succeed at the expense of the mind

The same mind that generates the unhealthy environment in which it struggles or succeeds

This is a grandiose lesson many may never learn but it is practical
Your thoughts are the things that hinder you in every sense
Especially the spiritual sense

As much as a single idea can bring fruition a cornucopia of creative movements for the better of self-improvement…

A hundred thoughts rooted in ego, self-serving, and traumatization
can and will bring destruction
Even to the best person who has the best intentions

Simply put…
Thoughts can hinder growth and development
Thoughts can destroy heart

The heart is the home to the spirit
That is what God intended upon our creation

Jesus knows what evils are in the heart of men due to the spirit
But we were not created with a bad heart simply because we were
not created with or even in a bad spirit

"Let Us make man in Our image" …

God is not bad nor evil

The tempter poisoned Adam and Eve with words
Words that affected the mind
Which in tune altered the heart

There were always those with good hearts put in positions despite
flaws so to speak… from Abraham to King David

Abraham had God in his heart…
Yet his mind was polluted with thoughts to proceed with his will
Bringing forth a seed against God's will
And as the Word says… Ishmael was born

King David saw Bathsheba…the rest is known
King David took a census… the rest is known

Stay afloat…

# Drifting Moments

Summertime in color
Champagne tears
Wasted
Tasted fears
Sounds of shapes
Basic
Success comes with a price
Washed away calm
The storm brews fresh ground
Keeps me wired…

Man…

Keeps me wired
Woke all night
Never sleeping…

Wait a minute…

Success comes with a price
If you don't pay attention
It will cost you twice over

Man…

Success comes with a price
Twice over
If you pay it no mind
Rice over chicken
Flipped backwards
Invest in memories
Drifting moments
Drift in brainstorms
Wash away pain
Refreshed by the clouds
Refreshing memories
Champagne tears difference
From the beginning

But the same
Celebrating both
Fresh French toast
Salmon in the sky
The fall and rise…

The fall and rise
Handwritten beautifully in disguise
In the skies
Footsteps in the dark
The marks left on the chalkboard
Dark night
Super Hero
Supreme Genius
The misdemeanor to miss demeanor of genius…

Whew…

Dark night
Super Hero
Supreme Genius
Saving lives from many lives away…

Ok…

Dark night
Super Hero
Supreme Genius
Blessing written on the blackboard in beautiful handwriting…

Man… got it together finally…

Dark night
Super Hero
Supreme Genius
Teaches lessons on a blackboard in disguise in the skies
Blessings to see such beautiful handwriting
The rise before sunrise
The fall after sun fall
Love is still the answer after all

Before you question anything
Question everything
Is it a crime?
The misdemeanor is to miss demeanor of genius

Beautiful lessons…

Teach us…

Jesus

God moves

# Wavy Days (Reprise)

Best believe walking on clouds
I can walk on water
I do it daily
Maybe more than that in other dimensions
Mentions of me motivate mountains to move
Splendor Slim groove
Written on Donnie's roof

Let me cut this off…

Let's cycle around to the aforementioned concept…
The 30/70
The concept of water and what it represents with us in our lives
The effect that it has
More so the destruction that it causes
The fear that it builds
The way that it can overwhelm…

Jesus told Peter to step out the boat
Join Him on the water
Peter finally heeded
Proceeded to step forth
However, he went back
In doing so Peter lost focus on Him
He reminded him on who He is, was, and always will be

You focus on the water and let it overtake you…
You will drown
You focus on God
You shall get the picture all the time
Whatever is going on in your life
At any given situation
Just remember to focus properly
And the water will wash away…

Maybe this will also help…
Some fresh deliberation moments

When I look at the ceiling fan
I see a proper perspective
I see past the blades right in front of me
I see past the light right in front of me
I see past what makes everyone cool
I see past that which brings everyone relief

I hone in on the ceiling itself
Right here is the most important of the fan
That is the base of the fan
The very foundation
This is what keeps everything secure:
The fan itself
The people under the fan
The very room where the fan is
It is securing everyone and everything within its presence

Here is more marvelous jewelry:
The ceiling fan gains its power from above
This power trickles down from the foundation above
Empowering the ceiling fan to keep everyone and everything cool below
In essence, the foundation of the fan keeps everyone and everything cool

Without this key component
The very thing is plain sight
That being the ceiling fan
Is useless

When the ceiling fan is inoperable
No one looks at the blades
No one looks at the lights
The focus then shifts to the base
The foundation that is above everything
The base becomes beta at best bet
The best bet responsible for existence in the first place

Why wait until things go bad in your eyes to focus on the foundation

Better answer…

Why disregard the foundation due to anything that is right in front of you…
Especially when you have been shown everything that is right in front of you…

It boils down to ego in a sense

Here's why:

God is only good enough to see when things go bad for you

God isn't good enough to see when things are going bad despite what He's done for you

God isn't Who He says He is despite saying I AM Who I AM

God can be disregard when you go through a little storm despite facts of His hand guiding you through storms and even sheltering you from storms

God empowered you, empowers you, and is empowering you

God has given you 30% of Himself to walk this green earth He made
The same green earth He utilized to make you

Gaining awareness of God and His acts
Gaining awareness of self
Gaining focus of God and of self
Maintaining awareness of God and His acts
Maintaining awareness of self
Maintaining focus of God and of self

There are no limits to achieving such
Actually there are 70 ways to achieve
70 paths to walk the right path and strive hard

Thank God for another day in the walk of the journey of life
Never be afraid to walk on water

# 88 Torahs…

God is the Supreme Genius…

- Fred "Benz" Merkerson

## Only Built 4 Champagne Thoughts…
## (God, Eric Walton)

Fresh Grapefruit

Champagne Mimosa Mornings

Bagels with the Smoked Salmon Cream Cheese

Fresh Flowers

Dogfights with the Red Baron

Wavy Days

Drifting Moments

Wavy Days (Reprise)

88 Torahs…

# Splendor Slim Groove
## (Introductory Outro)

I'm writing this here on 9/13/17 at 1:21 pm

A lot of things have occurred
A lot of life changes
A lot of times when you drift back and forth
You don't necessarily know where you are despite knowing and more so understanding where you are and have been

Drifting Moments is just what it reads as…
More like what it sounds like…
It sounds like I'm grappling with thoughts in my head as to what I am going through and what I am seeing

Nada and I moved here to Houston on April 15, 2017
In the time moving here
There has been a lot of interesting things to say the least…

The most interesting thing to happen to date is of course Hurricane Harvey

We came out of it relatively unscathed when you look at what could have happened compared to what did happen
Survivor's remorse… true that was there
But nothing was bigger and still being more prevalent than this being the final straw with Houston in the book of "we didn't sign up for this"

There has been a lot of deception to say the least
There has been a feeling of isolation
Albeit we are happy in our world that we have created
There is still the ongoing of realizing what we are living right now
There's the realization of how terrible this city is built
There is the realization of how deceitful people are
There is a disconnect with reality in a lot of ways

It took Hurricane Harvey to bring such to light to the point that you have no other reason but to notice it for what it is…

But in doing so…
You take away the focus from God
You make it about you
Even though it is truly about you and the move was made for betterment
You now have this to serve as a lesson and benchmark for what matters and what doesn't

As Jeremy would say in a paraphrase:
"E is very analytical… he's going to sit back through a bad event and make sense out of it"
It was good to spend time in Indiana with him this past Friday
Spend time with him and the others… just enjoy those who love you for you…
Not wanting anything else
Not being deceitful
Not being unwelcoming

Benz is also one of these people…
I built this book around that great quote that he told me over 2 years ago during a difficult time in life to say the least
I still remember where I was when he said it and it was one of those light bulb moments…
It summed up everything perfectly…the truth tends to do that all the time
It made me reflect upon everything
But it didn't bring understanding to everything instantly
It wasn't supposed to do so
And when I go through moments by myself, with Nada, or with others
I quote that line
I sit and expound on the matters that be
I reflect and gain wisdom
I strive towards understanding

I let God be God
Not that He needs my permission or anything…

But I pay homage to Him in stating that fact and seeing all that He has done…

In doing so I also study myself
I remember the fact that I am threefold as we all are
I remember that He has empowered me a long time ago

I am the essence of I AM

And God moves…

God moves…

Support the Arts:

The Rise with Love: Eric Walton in Rare Art Form

Splendid State of Mind

Splendid Clientele…

All can be found on Amazon.com and via a Google search of title and my name…

Peace and much gratitude to all…

www.ingramcontent.com/pod-product-compliance
Lightning Source LLC
Chambersburg PA
CBHW050248230526
45470CB00005B/2162